D0326027

Lent and Easter

with the Holy Fathers

Compiled by Peter Celano

PARACLETE PRESS
BREWSTER, MASSACHUSETTS

Lent and Easter with the Holy Fathers

2010 First Printing

Copyright © 2010 by Paraclete Press, Inc.

ISBN: 978-1-55725-692-8

Quotations from the Holy Scriptures, as used by the editor, are from the New Revised Standard Version Bible, copyright © 1989 by the Division of Christian Education of the National Council of the Churches of Christ in the United States of America, and are used by permission. All rights reserved.

Library of Congress Cataloging-in-Publication Data
Lent and Easter with the Holy Fathers / compiled by Peter Celano.
  p. cm.
 Includes bibliographical references.
 ISBN 978-1-55725-692-8 (hard cover)
1. Catholic Church--Prayers and devotions. 2. Lent--Prayers and devotions. 3. Easter--Prayers and devotions. I. Celano, Peter.
BX2170.L4L44 2010
 242'.34--dc22   2009046201

10 9 8 7 6 5 4 3 2 1

Published by Paraclete Press
Brewster, Massachusetts
www.paracletepress.com

Printed in the United States of America

CONTENTS

❧

LENT AND EASTER WITH THE HOLY FATHERS offers an opportunity for you to slow down and listen for God in this most important time of the Christian year. There is no more vital moment in our lives of faith than this one. Lent and Easter are when the essence of our faith is made manifest before our eyes. At this time of year, we are able to combine active participation in worship with personal study, prayer, and attentive listening for God's voice, learning anew how best to follow the One who died for us and then rose again.

Everything we do as Christians centers around this time of year. As Pope Clement XIII said in an encyclical from 1759 (quoted in detail below), Easter is the celebration "by which alone the dignity of all other religious occasions is consecrated." The Church would not exist if it were not for what happened on that first Easter Sunday. Also, the events of this season are all essentially connected: there would have been no Easter Sunday without Good Friday; Good Friday is best understood in the context of Palm Sunday; and the forty days of Lent begin for a variety of reasons at Ash Wednesday.

This is the story of the passion of our Lord. Our faith revolves around that passion, His death, and His resurrection. Without the events of this season, our faith wouldn't make any sense at all.

We usually think of this season of the Church year as a time for repentance and forgiveness, both interior and exterior. We devote ourselves more deliberately to prayer, reflection, study, making Confession, taking part in the Eucharistic sacrifice of Holy Communion, spending time in adoration of the Eucharist, and all other manner of observances of our Catholic faith.

We also rededicate ourselves to the Christian life by renouncing, or "giving up," certain things that have perhaps become too precious to us. We do these things in order to make amends for our own and other people's sins, and in the hope of the promise of everlasting love. In Galatians 5:24 St. Paul says:

> Those who belong to Christ Jesus have crucified the flesh with its passions and desires.

And as Pope John XXIII wrote in an encyclical from 1962:

Doing penance for one's sins is a first step towards obtaining forgiveness and winning eternal salvation. That is the clear and explicit teaching of Christ, and no one can fail to see how justified and how right the Catholic Church has always been in constantly insisting on this. She is the spokesman for her divine Redeemer. No individual Christian can grow in perfection, nor can Christianity gain in vigor, except it be on the basis of penance.[1]

So, many of us ever since childhood have identified the Lenten season with these two kinds of observances: interior and exterior. Both of these types of penance are important for the renewal of our religious lives.

Lent is not only about giving things up, but also about refocusing and rededicating. It is about the profound ways that we are reminded to turn again to God, to seek and find His loving presence ever closer in our Christian lives.

The second half of the title of this book is important as well: *with the Holy Fathers*. Popes past and present will be guiding us along this path, showing us what is most important, and encouraging us to allow God to fill much more of our lives than before.

Down through history, the personalities of the popes have varied widely, and each of them has had his own way of communicating and his own unique messages for the essential life of the Church in that day. The following collection of insights includes messages from Holy Fathers going back in history as far as St. Peter himself, and Pope St. Leo the Great, and also includes the teachings of other great saints from those earliest days. And then, of course, we have also included selections from a variety of other Holy Fathers throughout the ages, including several from our own Pope Benedict XVI, as well as from Pope John Paul II. We have provided the dates for each of the quotations from Pope Benedict and Pope John Paul II, for the benefit of readers who may even recall hearing their words on the occasions when they were first spoken.

You may have your own favorite pope in history— or perhaps one whose words of spiritual wisdom have most touched your heart—and we have tried to include as many of them as we could. You'll find the following in these pages:

- St. Peter (AD 30–64)
- Pope St. Leo the Great (440–61)

- Pope St. Gregory I (590–604)
- Pope Innocent III (1198–1216)
- Pope Clement XIII (1758–69)
- Pope Blessed Pius IX (1846–78)
- Pope Leo XIII (1878–1903)
- Pope Blessed John XXIII (1958–63)
- Pope John Paul II (1978–2005)
- Pope Benedict XVI (2005–)

The season of Lent has always been a special time for the Holy Fathers—their most profound meditations and reflections have come during this essential season in our lives. Pope John Paul II perhaps put it best when he said in 1979, during the first Lenten season of his pontificate: "The main current of Lent must flow through the interior man, through hearts and consciences. The essential effort of repentance consists in this. In this effort the human determination to be converted to God is invested with the predisposing grace of conversion and, at the same time, of forgiveness and of spiritual liberation."

We have included excerpts from as many of the papal homilies, encyclicals, and messages as we could. All of their messages are vital for the people of God, regardless of their denomination.

Again in the words of Pope John Paul II:

Dear Brothers and Sisters, let us set out with trust on our Lenten journey, sustained by fervent prayer, penance and concern for those in need. In particular, may this Lent be a time of ever greater concern for the needs of children, in our own families and in society as a whole: for they are the future of humanity.

With childlike simplicity let us turn to God and call him, as Jesus taught us in the prayer of the "Our Father," "Abba," "Father."

Our Father! Let us repeat this prayer often during Lent; let us repeat it with deep emotion. By calling God "Our Father," we will better realize that we are his children and feel that we are brothers and sisters of one another. Thus it will be easier for us to open our hearts to the little ones, following the invitation of Jesus: "Whoever receives one such child in my name receives me" (Mt. 18:5).

In this hope, I invoke upon each of you God's blessings, through the intercession of Mary, Mother of the Word of God made man and Mother of all humanity.

—*Message of His Holiness, John Paul II, for Lent* 2004

ONE

Shrove Tuesday

THE DAY BEFORE
THE HOLY SEASON OF LENT

*T*HIS DAY has two popular names: Shrove Tuesday and Fat Tuesday. We should say right at the beginning that Fat Tuesday (English for the French *Mardi gras*) is not on the Christian calendar. Fat Tuesday is not a liturgical feast. Far from it!

But Fat Tuesday is still an important aspect of Christian tradition, stemming back at least hundreds of years. This is the day that we remember we are only creatures. However, too often today this day before Ash Wednesday is marked by sinful, or at least imprudent, excesses and celebrations that are not at all mindful of the Lenten days to follow.

By tradition, the purpose of Fat Tuesday is to feast in order to mark the great difference between feasting and the fasting that begins the following morning. Traditionally, in old Europe and throughout Latin America even today, the feasting would consist of good wine, fattened calves, dairy, eggs, and cheese, and all manner of foods that should be gone from the cupboards and cellars before Lent begins. The parties in the French Quarter of New Orleans are what pops into many of our minds when we think of Fat Tuesday in the United States, and these are not the sort of celebrations that should mark the way that Christians spend the day before the season of Lent begins. But even in New Orleans, the streets are cleaned and the revelers pushed toward home—at midnight.

The origins of Fat Tuesday come from a time when the fasting of Lent was more deliberate and strict than it usually is today. It is uncommon today for Catholics to abstain from all wine, meat, and dairy products during the season of Lent. But such fasting is still encouraged, and it returns us to a better understanding of the purpose of this time of the year.

Given all of this complexity, let's call this day *Shrove Tuesday* instead. Shrove Tuesday focuses us on the specifically religious aspects of the day before Lent. *Shrove* comes from the old Anglo-Saxon verb *to shrive*, or "to make a confession," and to be *shriven*, or absolved of sins. This is the day when we finally make our spiritual preparations for the Lenten season that's upon us. In 1748, Pope Benedict XIV instituted what he called the "Forty Hours of Carnival" as an antidote to the excesses so often seen on Shrove Tuesday. Prayers were offered, the people were encouraged to make their confessions, and the Blessed Sacrament was exposed in parishes during the days leading up to Ash Wednesday. Still, in some parts of the world, these practices are a vibrant part of the "celebration" of this day before Lent.

PSALM 51

[In church, this is the last day of the liturgical calendar when Alleluias are supposed to be sung; they will now be put away for the next forty days. The Church reminds us that this day is supposed to be marked by waiting and a renewal of penitence, asking for God's mercy.]

Have mercy on me, O God,
  according to your steadfast love;
according to your abundant mercy
  blot out my transgressions.
Wash me thoroughly from my iniquity,
  and cleanse me from my sin.

For I know my transgressions,
  and my sin is ever before me.
Against you, you alone, have I sinned,
  and done what is evil in your sight,
so that you are justified in your sentence
  and blameless when you pass judgment.
Indeed, I was born guilty,
  a sinner when my mother conceived me.

You desire truth in the inward being;
  therefore teach me wisdom in my secret heart.
Purge me with hyssop, and I shall be clean;
  wash me, and I shall be whiter than snow.

Let me hear joy and gladness;
   let the bones that you have crushed rejoice.
Hide your face from my sins,
   and blot out all my iniquities.

Create in me a clean heart, O God,
   and put a new and right spirit within me.
Do not cast me away from your presence,
   and do not take your holy spirit from me.
Restore to me the joy of your salvation,
   and sustain in me a willing spirit.

Then I will teach transgressors your ways,
   and sinners will return to you.
Deliver me from bloodshed, O God,
      O God of my salvation,
   and my tongue will sing aloud of your
      deliverance.

O Lord, open my lips,
   and my mouth will declare your praise.
For you have no delight in sacrifice;
   if I were to give a burnt offering,
      you would not be pleased.
The sacrifice acceptable to God
      is a broken spirit;
   a broken and contrite heart, O God,
      you will not despise.

Do good to Zion in your good pleasure;
   rebuild the walls of Jerusalem,
then you will delight in right sacrifices,
   in burnt offerings and whole burnt offerings;
   then bulls will be offered on your altar.

A PRAYER FOR THE FORGIVENESS
OF SINS

*M*Y JESUS, I place all my sins before you. In my estimation they do not deserve pardon, but I ask you to close your eyes to my want of merit and open them to your infinite merit.

Since you willed to die for my sins, grant me forgiveness for all of them. Thus, I may no longer feel the burden of my sins, a burden that oppresses me beyond measure.

Assist me, dear Jesus, for I desire to become good no matter what the cost. Take away, destroy, and utterly root out whatever you find in me that is contrary to your holy will. At the same time, dear Jesus, illumine me so that I may walk in your holy light.

— ST. GEMMA GALGANI

St. Gemma Galgani was an Italian mystic and stigmatist who lived from 1878–1903. She was orphaned at the age of eighteen and lived a short life, becoming one of the most popular saints of the Passionist order. Her feast is celebrated on April 11.

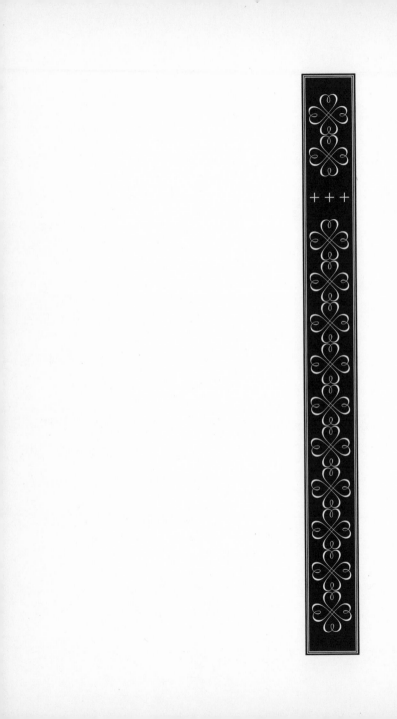

TWO

Ash Wednesday

AS POPE JOHN PAUL II said at the beginning of his 2004 Lenten message:

> The evocative rite of the imposition of ashes marks the beginning of the holy season of Lent, when the Liturgy once more calls the faithful to radical conversion and trust in God's mercy.

This is the day when the Lenten season officially begins.

Ash Wednesday is what is called a "moveable feast," which means that it falls on a different date each year because it's dependent on the date of Easter, which is also a moveable feast and is determined (ever since the Council of Nicaea in 325) as the first Sunday after the full moon (the Paschal Full Moon) following the vernal equinox. You're probably thinking that this sounds complicated, and you're right, but that's why most of us simply look to the many published liturgical calendars to find when Lent begins. Ash Wednesday can occur as early as February 4, or as late as March 10.

This is the day that our priest smears ashes on our foreheads, reminding us that we are dust. The symbolism of ashes is something that Christians inherited from Judaism. Throughout the Hebrew Scriptures we see instances of the People of Israel using ashes to show their repentance—as when the King of Nineveh listened to the prophecy of Jonah:

Jonah began to go into the city, going a day's walk. And he cried out, "Forty days more, and Nineveh shall be overthrown!" And the people of Nineveh believed God; they proclaimed a fast, and everyone, great and small, put on sackcloth.

When the news reached the king of Nineveh, he rose from his throne, removed his robe, covered himself with sackcloth, and sat in ashes. Then he had a proclamation made in Nineveh: "By the decree of the king and his nobles: No human being or animal, no herd or flock, shall taste anything. They shall not feed, nor shall they drink water. Human beings and animals shall be covered with sackcloth, and they shall cry mightily to God. All shall turn from their evil ways and from the violence that is in their hands. Who knows? God may relent and change his mind; he may turn from his fierce anger, so that we do not perish."

When God saw what they did, how they turned from their evil ways, God changed his mind about the calamity that he had said he would bring upon them; and he did not do it.

—JONAH 3:4-10

Ash Wednesday also connects us to our Lord, who went into the desert for forty days to be tempted by the Evil One. In these forty days of our own "desert" time, we refocus on Christ's redeeming work and the promise of resurrection. In the cycle of the church year, then, Ash Wednesday connects us to His passion as we remembered it last year, as the ashes that are smeared onto our foreheads today, reminding us of our mortality, are made from the palms that we used to process into "Jerusalem" last year as we celebrated Palm Sunday.

TWO SCRIPTURES WE HEAR ON ASH WEDNESDAY

By the sweat of your face
    you shall eat bread
until you return to the ground,
    for out of it you were taken;
you are dust,
    and to dust you shall return.
        —GENESIS 3:19

The time is fulfilled, and the kingdom of God has come near; repent, and believe in the good news.
        —MARK 1:15

CELEBRATING THE SAVING WORK
OF GOD

*H*OLY MOTHER CHURCH believes that she should celebrate the saving work of her divine Spouse in a sacred commemoration on certain days throughout the course of the year. Once each week, on the day which she has called the Lord's Day, she keeps the memory of the Lord's resurrection. She also celebrates it once every year, together with his blessed Passion, at Easter, that most solemn of all feasts. In the course of the year, moreover, she unfolds the whole mystery of Christ. . . . Thus recalling the mysteries of the redemption, she opens up to the faithful the riches of her Lord's powers and merits, so that these are in some way made present in every age; the faithful lay hold of them and are filled with saving grace.

—*The Catechism of the Catholic Church*,
paragraph #1163

Calls to Penance in the Bible

 POPE JOHN XXIII

from the encyclical Paenitentiam Agere

NOW WE HAVE ONLY to open the sacred books of the Old and New Testament to be assured of one thing: it was never God's will to reveal Himself in any solemn encounter with mortal men—to speak in human terms—without first calling them to prayer and penance. Indeed, Moses refused to give the Hebrews the tables of the Law until they had expiated their crime of idolatry and ingratitude.

So too the Prophets; they never wearied of exhorting the Israelites to make their prayers acceptable to God, their supreme Overlord, by offering them in a penitential spirit. Otherwise they would bring about their own exclusion from the plan of divine Providence, according to which God Himself was to be the King of His chosen people.

The most deeply impressive of these prophetic utterances is surely that warning of Joel which is constantly ringing in our ears in the course of the Lenten liturgy: "Now therefore, says the Lord, Be converted to me with all your heart, in fasting and in weeping and in mourning. And rend your hearts and not your garments. . . . Between the porch and the altar the priests, the Lord's ministers, shall weep and say: Spare, O Lord, spare thy people, and give not thy inheritance to reproach, that the heathen should rule over them."

Nor did these calls to penance cease when the Son of God became incarnate. On the contrary, they became even more insistent. At the very outset of his preaching, John the Baptist proclaimed: "Do penance, for the kingdom of heaven is at hand." And Jesus inaugurated His saving mission in the same way. He did not begin by revealing the principal truths of the faith. First He insisted that the soul must repent of every trace of sin that could render it impervious to the message of eternal salvation: "From that time Jesus began to preach and to say, Do penance, for the kingdom of heaven is at hand."

He was even more vehement than were the Prophets in His demands that those who listened to Him should undergo a complete change of heart and submit in perfect sincerity to all the laws of the Supreme God. "For behold," He said, "the kingdom of God is within you."

The Apostles held undeviatingly to the principles of their divine Master. When the Holy Spirit had descended on them in the form of fiery tongues, Peter expressed his invitation to the multitudes to seek rebirth in Christ and to accept the gifts of the most holy Paraclete in these words: "Do penance and be baptized, every one of you, in the name of Jesus Christ, for the remission of your sins. And you will receive the gift of the Holy Spirit." Paul too, the teacher of the Gentiles, announced to the Romans in no uncertain terms that the kingdom of God did not consist in an attitude of intellectual superiority or in indulging the pleasures of sense. It consisted in the triumph of justice and in peace of mind. "For the kingdom of God does not consist in food and drink, but in justice and peace and joy in the Holy Spirit."

"Your Father who sees in secret will reward you"
(Mt. 6:4, 6, 18)

POPE JOHN PAUL II
Ash Wednesday Homily
February 25, 2004

*J*ESUS' WORDS are addressed to each one of us at the beginning of our Lenten journey. We begin it with the imposition of ashes, an austere penitential gesture very dear to Christian tradition. It emphasizes the awareness of sinners as they stand before the majesty and holiness of God. At the same time, it demonstrates readiness to accept and to transform into concrete choices adherence to the Gospel.

The formulas that accompany it are very eloquent. The first, from the Book of Genesis: "You are dust, and to dust you shall return" (Gen. 3:19), calls to mind the present human condition, marked by transitoriness and limitation. The second one takes up the words of the Gospel: "Repent and believe in the Gospel" (Mk. 1:15), which are a pressing appeal to change one's life. Both these formulas invite us to enter Lent in an attitude of listening and sincere conversion.

The Path to Holiness

POPE JOHN PAUL II
Ash Wednesday Homily
February 25, 2004

THE GOSPEL emphasizes that the Lord "sees in secret," that is, he scrutinizes our hearts. The external gestures of penance are valuable if they are an expression of an inner attitude and demonstrate the firm determination to shun evil and to take the path of righteousness. This is the profound sense of Christian ascesis.

Ascesis: the very word evokes the image of ascending to lofty heights. This necessarily entails sacrifices and renunciation. Indeed, to make the journey easier, one must be reduced to the bare essentials; to be prepared to face every hardship and overcome every obstacle in order to reach the pre-established goal. To become authentic disciples of Christ, it is necessary to deny oneself, take up one's cross and follow him (cf. Lk. 9:23). This is the arduous path to holiness that every baptized person is called to follow.

The Church has always pointed out certain useful means for taking this route. They consist above all in humble and docile adherence to God's will accompanied by ceaseless prayer; they are the typical forms of penance of Christian tradition, such as abstinence, fasting, mortification and giving up even good things legitimate in themselves; they are the concrete acts of acceptance of our neighbor that are referred to in today's Gospel with the term "giving alms." All these things are suggested once again but with greater intensity during the season of Lent, which in this regard is a "strong moment" for spiritual training and generous service to our brothers and sisters.

Who needs protection more than a frail, defenseless child?

A PRAYER FOR TRUE DEVOTION

*H*UMBLE YOURSELF PROFOUNDLY before God, saying from your heart, with the Psalmist, "O Lord! my whole being is as nothing before You, and how have You remembered me to create me?" O my soul, you were engulfed in that ancient nothing, and had God not drawn you to Himself, what would you have done in that barren state?

Return thanks to God. O my great and good Creator, how much I am obliged to You, since You chose to draw me out of nothing, in Your mercy to make me what I am? What can I ever do to bless Your holy name as I should, and to render thanks to Your inestimable goodness?

—ST. FRANCIS DE SALES
from Introduction to a Devout Life

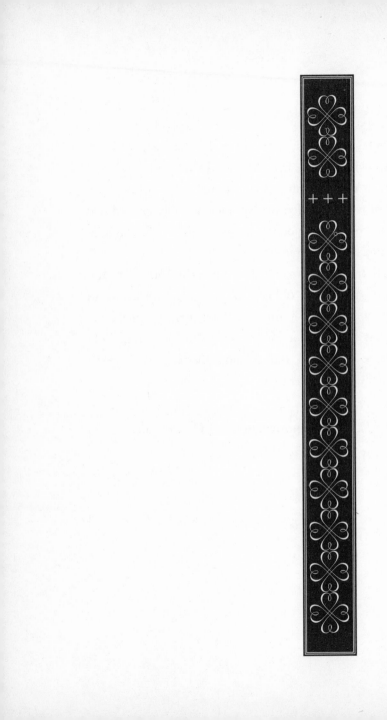

THREE

Forty Days of Preparation

*A*FTER ASH WEDNESDAY, Lent continues for forty-six days until Easter Sunday. We traditionally think of Lent as lasting only forty days—and this is true—because technically we don't count Sundays as Lenten days. Strictly speaking, Lent lasts forty days from Ash Wednesday to Easter Sunday, because the Sundays are excluded. It's impossible to be sorrowful on the Lord's Day, and we still celebrate the resurrection at Mass each Sunday!

These are days for prayer, spiritual discipline, self-denial, and reflection on the saving grace of God. We are supposed to enter into this time in the spirit of walking together with Christ through His preparation and His passion, and toward the cross and the resurrection. These are days of our fullest expression of what it means to follow Jesus!

We choose to observe these prayerful days in a variety of ways. For instance, we don't eat meat on Fridays. Why is that? These practices have evolved over the centuries. In the late Middle Ages, St. Thomas Aquinas wrote about the importance of abstaining from eating all animal products during Lent, so as to avoid foods that might incite lustful or passionate feelings. Today, we understand differently the way foods impact our bodies, but the principle still remains: simplicity and self-denial.

The Gospels say that Jesus fasted in the desert for those forty days that he was tempted. We should do likewise during these days to be reminded more often of the sacrifice that Christ made for us alone.

Living the Love of Christ

POPE JOHN PAUL II
Message for Lent 1998

*D*EAR BROTHERS AND SISTERS! Each year Lent recalls the mystery of Christ "led by the Spirit in the desert" (Lk. 4:1). With this unique experience, Jesus gave witness to His complete surrender to the will of the Father. The Church offers the faithful this liturgical season so that they can renew themselves internally through the Word of God and may express in life the love which Christ instills in the heart of everyone who believes in Him.

The Blessings of Abstinence

POPE ST. GREGORY I
from his Dialogues

LONG AGO, A NOBLEMAN named Venantius lived in the country of Samnium, and this farmer had a son called Honoratus, who from his childhood thirsted after the joys of heaven by the virtue of abstinence. In all things he led a holy life, refraining from all idle talk and subduing his body by means of abstinence. His parents, upon a certain day, had invited their neighbors to a banquet which consisted completely of flesh. But because of the love of mortification, Honoratus refused to eat. His father and mother began to laugh at him, willing him to do as they themselves were doing and eat the meat: "For where can we," they joked, "get you any fish here in these mountains?" (In that place they used to sometimes hear of fish, but seldom see any.) And while they were still jesting and mocking their son, suddenly they lacked water. A servant with a wooden bucket went to the well to fetch some, and into the bucket, as he was a drawing the water, a fish entered in. Upon the servant's return, together with the water, he poured forth before them all a great fish, and it served Honoratus very well for all of that day. At this strange turn of events, all present were struck in admiration, and Honoratus' parents themselves began to abstain from any more scoffing at the boy's virtue, and began to revere his abstinence.

*"Whoever receives one such child in my name
receives me." (Mt. 18:5)*

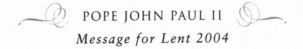

POPE JOHN PAUL II
Message for Lent 2004

*T*HIS YEAR'S THEME invites us to reflect on the
condition of children. Today Jesus continues to call
them to himself and to set them as an example to all
those who wish to be his disciples. Jesus' words call
upon us to see how children are treated in our families,
in civil society, and in the Church. They are also an
incentive to rediscover the simplicity and trust which
believers must cultivate in imitation of the Son of
God, who shared the lot of the little ones and the
poor. Saint Clare of Assisi loved to say that Christ
"lay in a manger, lived in poverty on the earth and
died naked on the Cross" (*Testament, Franciscan Sources*,
No. 2841).

Jesus had a particular love for children because of
"their simplicity, their joy of life, their spontaneity,
and their faith filled with wonder" (*Angelus Message*,
December 18, 1994). For this reason he wishes the
community to open its arms and its heart to them,
even as he did: "Whoever receives one such child in my
name receives me" (Mt. 18:5). Alongside children Jesus
sets the "very least of the brethren": the suffering, the

needy, the hungry and thirsty, strangers, the naked, the sick, and the imprisoned. In welcoming them and loving them, or in treating them with indifference and contempt, we show our attitude towards him, for it is in them that he is particularly present.

The Gospel recounts the childhood of Jesus in the simple home of Nazareth, where he was obedient to his parents and "increased in wisdom and in years, and in favor with God and man" (Lk. 2:52). By becoming himself a child, he wished to share our human experience. "He emptied himself," writes the Apostle Paul, "taking the form of a slave, being born in the likeness of men. And being found in human form he humbled himself and became obedient unto death, even death on a Cross" (Phil. 2:7–8). When at twelve years old he remained in the Temple in Jerusalem, he said to his parents who anxiously looked for him: "How is it that you sought me? Did you not know that I must be in my Father's house?" (Lk. 2:49). Indeed, his whole life was marked by a trusting and filial obedience to his heavenly Father. "My food," he said, "is to do the will of him who sent me, and to accomplish his work" (Jn. 4:34).

In the years of his public life Jesus often insisted that only those who become like children will enter the Kingdom of Heaven (cf. Mt. 18:3; Mk. 10:15; Lk. 18:17; Jn. 3:3). In his teaching, young children become a striking image of the disciple who is called to follow the divine Master with childlike docility: "Whoever humbles himself like this child, he is the greatest in the Kingdom of Heaven" (Mt. 18:4).

"To become" one of the least and "to receive" the little ones: these are two aspects of a single teaching which the Lord repeats to his disciples in our time. Only the one who makes himself one of the "least" is able to receive with love the "least" of our brothers and sisters.

Mystery and Fasting

POPE CLEMENT XIII

from his encyclical Appetente Sacro

THE HOLY SEASON OF LENT . . . is full of
mysteries but not without mystery. It precedes that
great celebration of Easter, by which alone the
dignity of all other religious occasions is consecrated.
Venerable Brothers, you should see that the faithful
religiously observe this holy fast, which was
recommended by the testimony of the laws and the
prophets, consecrated by the Lord Jesus Christ, and
handed on by the apostles. The Catholic Church has
always preserved it so that by the mortification of
the flesh and the humiliation of the spirit, we might
be better prepared to approach the mysteries of the
Lord's passion and the paschal sacraments. Likewise
through fasting we might rise again in the resurrection
of Him whose passion and death we joined after we
put off the old man.

FORTY DAYS IN THE DESERT

*T*HE FORTY DAYS' FAST which we call Lent is the Church's preparation for Easter, and was instituted at the very commencement of Christianity. Our blessed Lord Himself sanctioned it by fasting forty days and forty nights in the desert; and though He would not impose it on the world by an express commandment (which, in that case, could not have been open to the power of dispensation), yet He showed plainly enough, by His own example, that fasting, which God had so frequently ordered in the old Law, was to be also practiced by the children of the new.

The disciples of St. John the Baptist came, one day, to Jesus, and said to Him: "Why do we and the Pharisees fast often, but Thy disciples do not fast?" And Jesus said to them: "Can the children of the Bridegroom mourn, as long as the Bridegroom is with them? But the days will come, when the Bridegroom shall be taken away from them, and then they shall fast" (Mt. 9:14–15).

Hence we find it mentioned, in the Acts of the Apostles, how the disciples of our Lord, after the foundation of the Church, applied themselves to fasting. In their Epistles, also, they recommended it to the faithful.

—DOM GUERANGER, O.S.B.
from "The History of Lent"[2]

FASTING: A MEANS OF GRACE

"He fasted for forty days and forty nights, and afterwards he was famished." (Mt. 4:2)

*T*HE SEASON OF HUMILIATION, which precedes Easter, lasts for forty days, in memory of our Lord's long fast in the wilderness. Accordingly on this day, the first Sunday in Lent, we read the Gospel which gives an account of it; and in the Collect we pray Him, who for our sakes fasted forty days and forty nights, to bless our abstinence to the good of our souls and bodies.

We fast by way of penitence, and in order to subdue the flesh. Our Savior had no need of fasting for either purpose. His fasting was unlike ours, as in its intensity, so in its object. And yet when we begin to fast, His pattern is set before us; and we continue the time of fasting till, in number of days, we have equaled His. There is a reason for this; in truth, we must do nothing except with Him in our eye. As He it is, through whom alone we have the power to do any good thing, so unless we do it for Him it is not good. From Him our obedience comes, towards Him it must look. He says, "Without Me ye can do nothing" (John 15:5). No work is good without grace and without love.

St. Paul gave up all things "to be found in Christ not having his own righteousness which is of the law but the righteousness which is from God upon faith" (Phil. 3:9). Then only are our righteousnesses acceptable when they are done, not in a legal way, but in Christ through faith. Vain were all the deeds of the Law, because they were not attended by the power of the Spirit. They were the mere attempts of unaided nature to fulfill what it ought indeed, but was not able to fulfil. . . .

But God hath reserved some better thing for us. This is what it is to be one of Christ's little ones, to be able to do what the Jews thought they could do, and could not; to have that within us through which we can do all things; to be possessed by His presence as our life, our strength, our merit, our hope, our crown; to become in a wonderful way His members, the instruments, or visible form, or sacramental sign, of the One Invisible Ever-Present Son of God, mystically reiterating in each of us all the acts of His earthly life, His birth, consecration, fasting, temptation, conflicts, victories, sufferings, agony, passion, death, resurrection, and ascension;—He being all in all, we, with as little power in ourselves, as little excellence or merit, as the water in Baptism, or the bread and wine in Holy Communion, yet strong in the Lord and in the power of His might. These are the thoughts with which we celebrated Christmas and Epiphany, these are the thoughts which must accompany us through Lent. Yes, even in our penitential exercises, when we could least have hoped to find a pattern in Him, Christ has gone before us to sanctify them to us. He has blessed fasting as a means of grace, in that He has fasted; and fasting is only acceptable when it is done for His sake.

—BLESSED JOHN HENRY CARDINAL
NEWMAN (1801–90)
from a Sermon for the First Sunday of Lent

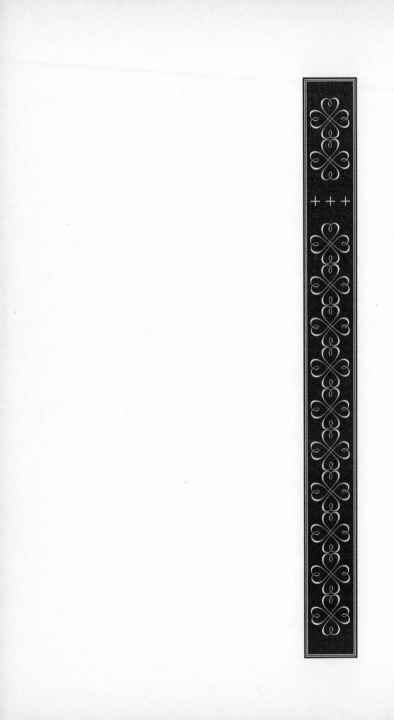

FOUR

Holy Week

THESE ESSENTIAL DAYS

*T*HIS IS THE MOST POIGNANT WEEK in our lives—the most important week in the history of the world. Each year, we relive the events of what happened 2,000 years ago, and we are powerfully reminded of the sacrifice and love of our Lord.

As Pope John Paul II said in his 2004 Lenten message: "During Lent, we prepare to relive the Paschal Mystery, which sheds the light of hope upon the whole of our existence, even its most complex and painful aspects. Holy Week will again set before us this mystery of salvation in the evocative rites of the Easter Triduum."

POPE ST. LEO THE GREAT
from his Sermon on the Beatitudes

WHEN OUR LORD JESUS CHRIST was preaching the Gospel of the kingdom and healing various illnesses throughout the whole of Galilee, the fame of his mighty works spread into all of Syria, and great crowds from all parts of Judea flocked to the heavenly physician. Because human ignorance is slow to believe what it does not see, and equally slow to hope for what it does not know, those who were to be instructed in the divine teaching had first to be aroused by bodily benefits and visible miracles so that, once they had experienced his gracious power, they would no longer doubt the wholesome effect of his doctrine.

In order, therefore, to transform outward healings into inward remedies, and to cure men's souls now that he had healed their bodies, our Lord separated himself from the surrounding crowds, climbed to the solitude of a neighboring mountain, and called the apostles to himself. From the height of this mystical site he then instructed them in the most lofty doctrines, suggesting both by the very nature of the place and by what he was doing that it was he who long ago had honored Moses by speaking to him. At that time, his words showed a terrifying justice, but now they reveal a sacred compassion, in order to fulfill what was promised in the words of the prophet Jeremiah: "Behold the days are coming, says the Lord, when I shall establish a new covenant with the house of Israel and with the house of Judah. After those days, says the Lord, I shall put my laws within them and write them on their hearts."

And so it was that he who had spoken to Moses spoke also to the apostles. Writing in the hearts of his disciples, the swift hand of the Word composed the ordinances of the new covenant. And this was not done as formerly, in the midst of dense clouds, amid terrifying sounds and lightning, so that the people were frightened away from approaching the mountain. Instead, there was a tranquil discourse which clearly reached the ears of all who stood nearby so that the harshness of the law might be softened by the gentleness of grace, and the spirit of adoption might dispel the terror of slavery.

Concerning the content of Christ's teaching, his own sacred words bear witness: whoever longs to attain eternal happiness can now recognize the steps that lead to that high state. "Blessed," he says, "are the poor in spirit, for theirs is the kingdom of heaven." It might have been unclear to which poor he was referring, if after the words "Blessed are the poor," he had not added anything about the kind of poor he had in mind. For then the poverty that many suffer because of grave and harsh necessity might seem sufficient to merit the kingdom of heaven.

But when he says: "Blessed are the poor in spirit," he shows that the kingdom of heaven is to be given to those who are distinguished by their humility of soul rather than by their lack of worldly goods.

PALM SUNDAY

ALL FOUR OF THE GOSPELS tell of Jesus' march into Jerusalem the Sunday before Resurrection Sunday. The people who watched this procession sang words from Psalm 118 that we still sing each week at Mass. You will notice the verse from this passage:

BLESSED IS HE WHO COMES IN THE NAME OF THE LORD

Blessed is the one who comes in the
     name of the LORD.
  We bless you from the house of the LORD.
The LORD is God,
  and he has given us light.
Bind the festal procession with branches,
  up to the horns of the altar.

You are my God, and I will give thanks to you;
  you are my God, I will extol you.

O give thanks to the LORD, for he is good,
  for his steadfast love endures for ever.
      —PSALM 118:26–29

Celebration of Palm Sunday of the Passion of Our Lord

POPE BENEDICT XVI

St. Peter's Square, April 5, 2009

TOGETHER WITH A GROWING MULTITUDE of pilgrims, Jesus had gone up to Jerusalem for the Passover. In the final stage of the journey, near Jericho, he had healed blind Bartimaeus, who called upon him as Son of David, pleading for mercy. Now—having received his sight—he had gratefully joined the group of pilgrims. At the gates of Jerusalem, when Jesus sat upon a donkey, an animal symbolizing the Davidic kingship, there spontaneously arose among the pilgrims the joyful conviction: It is He, the Son of David! Accordingly, they greet Jesus with the messianic acclamation: "Blessed is he who comes in the name of the Lord," and they add: "Blessed is the kingdom of our father David that is coming! Hosanna in the highest!" (Mk. 11:9). We do not know exactly what the enthusiastic pilgrims imagined the coming kingdom of David would be like. But what about us, have we truly understood the message of Jesus, the Son of David? Have we grasped what is meant by the Kingdom of which He speaks during his interrogation with Pilate? Do we understand what it means to say that this Kingdom is not of this world? Or would we actually prefer that it were of this world?

MAUNDY THURSDAY

*A*MONG THE MOST POWERFUL moments that we
relive this week are those events of the night before
He was arrested: what we today call *Maundy Thursday*,
when Jesus showed His disciples what it meant to be
a servant-leader. No one knows for certain why the
English word "Maundy" became attached to this day,
but it may be from the Latin word *mandatum*, which is
the first word of this verse from St. John's Gospel that
Christ taught to His disciples:

> I give you a new commandment, that you love one
> another. Just as I have loved you, you also should love
> one another.
>
> —JOHN 13:34

He came to Simon Peter, who said to him, "Lord, are you going to wash my feet?" Jesus answered, "You do not know now what I am doing, but later you will understand." Peter said to him, "You will never wash my feet." Jesus answered, "Unless I wash you, you have no share with me." Simon Peter said to him, "Lord, not my feet only but also my hands and my head!"

—JOHN 13:6–9

THE LORD'S SUPPER

*"Having loved his own who were in the world,
he loved them to the end." (Jn. 13:1)*

POPE BENEDICT XVI
Holy Thursday Mass, April 13, 2006

GOD LOVES HIS CREATURE, man; he even loves
him in his fall and does not leave him to himself. He
loves him to the end. He is impelled with his love to
the very end, to the extreme: he came down from his
divine glory.

He cast aside the raiment of his divine glory and put
on the garb of a slave. He came down to the extreme
lowliness of our fall. He kneels before us and carries
out for us the service of a slave: he washes our dirty
feet so that we might be admitted to God's banquet
and be made worthy to take our place at his table—
something that on our own we neither could nor
would ever be able to do.

God is not a remote God, too distant or too great
to be bothered with our trifles. Since God is great, he
can also be concerned with small things. Since he is
great, the soul of man, the same man, created through
eternal love, is not a small thing but great, and worthy
of God's love.

God's holiness is not merely an incandescent power before which we are obliged to withdraw, terrified. It is a power of love and therefore a purifying and healing power.

God descends and becomes a slave, he washes our feet so that we may come to his table. In this, the entire mystery of Jesus Christ is expressed. In this, what redemption means becomes visible.

The basin in which he washes us is his love, ready to face death. Only love has that purifying power which washes the grime from us and elevates us to God's heights.

The basin that purifies us is God himself, who gives himself to us without reserve—to the very depths of his suffering and his death. He is ceaselessly this love that cleanses us; in the sacraments of purification— Baptism and the Sacrament of Penance—he is continually on his knees at our feet and carries out for us the service of a slave, the service of purification, making us capable of God.

His love is inexhaustible, it truly goes to the very end.

"You are clean, but not all of you," the Lord says (Jn. 13:10). This sentence reveals the great gift of purification that he offers to us, because he wants to be at table together with us, to become our food. "But not all of you"—the obscure mystery of rejection exists, which becomes apparent with Judas' act, and precisely on Holy Thursday, the day on which Jesus made the gift of himself, it should give us food for thought. The Lord's love knows no bounds, but man can put a limit on it.

"You are clean, but not all of you" (Jn. 13:10)

POPE BENEDICT XVI
Holy Thursday Mass, April 13, 2006

WHAT IS IT THAT MAKES MAN UNCLEAN?

It is the rejection of love, not wanting to be loved, not loving. It is pride that believes it has no need of any purification, that is closed to God's saving goodness. It is pride that does not want to admit or recognize that we are in need of purification.

In Judas we see the nature of this rejection even more clearly. He evaluated Jesus in accordance with the criteria of power and success. For him, power and success alone were real; love did not count. And he was greedy: money was more important than communion with Jesus, more important than God and his love.

He thus also became a liar who played a double game and broke with the truth; one who lived in deceit and so lost his sense of the supreme truth, of God. In this way, he became hard of heart and incapable of conversion, of the trusting return of the Prodigal Son, and he disposed of the life destroyed.

"You are clean, but not all of you." Today, the Lord alerts us to the self-sufficiency that puts a limit on his unlimited love. He invites us to imitate his humility, to entrust ourselves to it, to let ourselves be "infected" by it.

He invites us—however lost we may feel—to return home, to let his purifying goodness uplift us and enable us to sit at table with him, with God himself.

Let us add a final word to this inexhaustible Gospel passage: "For I have given you an example" (Jn. 13:15); "You also ought to wash one another's feet" (Jn. 13:14). Of what does "washing one another's feet" consist? What does it actually mean?

This: every good work for others—especially for the suffering and those not considered to be worth much—is a service of the washing of feet.

The Lord calls us to do this: to come down, learn humility and the courage of goodness, and also the readiness to accept rejection and yet to trust in goodness and persevere in it.

But there is another, deeper dimension. The Lord removes the dirt from us with the purifying power of his goodness. Washing one another's feet means above all tirelessly forgiving one another, beginning together ever anew, however pointless it may seem. It means purifying one another by bearing with one another and by being tolerant of others; purifying one another, giving one another the sanctifying power of the Word of God and introducing one another into the Sacrament of divine love.

The Lord purifies us, and for this reason we dare to approach his table. Let us pray to him to give to all of us the grace of being able to one day be guests for ever at the eternal nuptial banquet. Amen!

GOOD FRIDAY

*T*HIS IS THE SOLEMN DAY that we remember Christ's death upon the cross.

The Cross and the Meaning of It

POPE ST. LEO THE GREAT
Homily on the Passion of Christ

*C*HRIST HAS BEEN LIFTED UP upon the cross, so let the eyes of your mind dwell not only on that sight which those wicked sinners saw, to whom it was said by the mouth of Moses, "And thy life shall be hanging before your eyes, and you shall fear day and night, and shall not be assured of thy life." For in the crucified Lord they could think of nothing but their wicked deed, having not the fear by which true faith is justified, but that by which an evil conscience is racked.

Let our understandings, illumined by the Spirit of Truth, foster with pure and free heart the glory of the cross which irradiates heaven and earth, and see with the inner sight what the Lord meant when he spoke of his coming Passion: "The hour is come that the Son of man may be glorified"; and then when he says, "Now is My spirit troubled. And what shall I say? Father, save Me from this hour, but for this cause came I unto this hour. Father, glorify Thy Son." The Father's voice came from heaven, saying, "I have both glorified it and will glorify it again," and Jesus said in reply to those that stood nearby: "This voice came not for Me but for you. Now is the world's judgment, now shall the prince of this world be cast out. And I, if I be lifted up from the earth, will draw all things unto Me."

The Power of the Cross Is Universally Attractive

POPE ST. LEO THE GREAT
Homily on the Passion of Christ

O WONDROUS POWER OF THE CROSS! *O* ineffable glory of the Passion, in which is contained the Lord's tribunal, the world's judgment, and the power of the Crucified! For you drew all things unto yourself, Lord, and when you had stretched out your hands, to an unbelieving people that had forgotten you, the whole world at last was brought to confess your majesty.

You drew all things unto yourself, Lord, when all the elements combined to pronounce judgment . . . when the lights of heaven were darkened, and the day turned into night, and the earth also was shaken . . . and all creation refused to serve those wicked ones. You drew all things unto yourself, Lord. The veil of the temple was rent, and the Holy of Holies existed no more for those unworthy high-priests. Falsity was turned into Truth, prophecy into Revelation, Law into Gospel. You drew all things unto yourself, Lord, so that what was done before in one temple was now to be celebrated everywhere by the piety of all the nations in full openness. For now there is a nobler rank of Levites, there are elders of greater dignity and priests of holier anointing: because your cross is the fount of all blessings, the source of all graces, and through it the believers receive strength for weakness, glory for shame, life for death. Now, too, the variety of fleshly sacrifices has ceased, and the one offering of Thy Body and Blood fulfils all those different victims: for Thou art the true "Lamb of God, that takes away the sins of the world," and in you were accomplished all mysteries. Now, there is only one sacrifice instead of many victims, so that there is but one kingdom instead of many nations.

ST. ALPHONSUS LIGUORI
from "A Prayer to Jesus in the Blessed Sacrament"

My Lord Jesus Christ,
who for the love You bear toward humankind,
remain night and day in this Sacrament,
all full of tenderness and love, expecting,
inviting and receiving all those who come to
    visit You:
I believe that You are present in the Sacrament of the
    altar;
I adore You from the depths of my own
    nothingness
and thank You for all the favors You have
    bestowed upon me;
and especially for having given me Yourself
    in this Sacrament,
and Your most holy Mother Mary as
    my advocate;
and for having called me to visit You in this church.

St. Alphonsus Liguori (1696–1787) was a Neapolitan bishop, writer, and teacher, known for his insightfulness and the power of his prayer. In 1732 he became the founder of the Congregation of the Most Holy Redeemer, known today as the "Redemptorists." Pope Gregory XVI made St. Alphonsus a Doctor of the Church.

POPE JOHN PAUL II
Easter Vigil Homily, April 14, 1979

THIS IS THE NIGHT of the Great Awaiting. Let us wait in Faith, let us wait with all our human being for him who at dawn broke the tyranny of death and revealed the Divine Power of Life: he is our Hope.

The Silence of Holy Saturday

POPE JOHN PAUL II

Easter Vigil Homily, April 14, 1979

ALTHOUGH HUMANITY HAS, during so many generations, become accustomed in a way to the reality of death and to its inevitability, it is, however, something overwhelming every time.

Christ's death had entered deeply the hearts of those closest to him, and the consciousness of the whole of Jerusalem. The silence that followed it filled the Friday evening and the whole of the following Saturday. On this day, in accordance with Jewish regulations, no one had gone to the place of his burial. The three women, of whom today's Gospel speaks, well remember the heavy stone with which the entrance to the sepulcher had been closed. This stone, of which they were thinking and about which they would speak the next day on their way to the sepulcher, also symbolizes the weight that had crushed their hearts. The stone that had separated the Dead One from the living, the stone that marked the limit of life, the weight of death. The women, who go to the sepulcher in the early morning of the day after the Sabbath, will not speak of death, but of the stone.

When they arrive at the spot, they will see that the stone no longer blocks the entrance to the sepulcher. It has been rolled back. They will not find Jesus in the sepulcher. They looked for him in vain! "He is not here; for he has risen, as he said" (Mt. 28:6). They are to go back to the city and announce to the disciples that he has risen again and that they will see him in Galilee. The women are not able to utter a word. The news of death is spoken in a low voice. The words of the resurrection were even difficult for them to grasp. Difficult to repeat, so much has the reality of death influenced man's thought and heart.

[Editor's note: The reflection that follows is a continuation of the one that precedes it.]

The Paschal Vigil. The Paschal Joy!

POPE JOHN PAUL II
Easter Vigil Homily, April 14, 1979

SINCE THAT NIGHT and even more so since
that morning which followed it, Christ's disciples
have learned to utter the word "resurrection." And
it has become the most important word, the central
word, the fundamental word in their language.
Everything takes its origin again from it. Everything
is confirmed and is constructed again: "The stone
which the builders rejected has become the chief
cornerstone. This is the Lord's doing; it is marvellous in
our eyes. This is the day which the Lord has made: let
us rejoice and be glad in it" (Psalm 117[118]:22–24).

It is for this very reason that the paschal vigil—the
day following Good Friday—is no longer only the
day on which the word "death" is spoken in a low
voice, on which the last moments of the life of the
Dead Man are remembered: it is the day of a great
Awaiting. It is the Easter Vigil: the day and the
night of waiting for the Day which the Lord has
made.

The liturgical content of the Vigil is expressed by
means of the various hours of the breviary and is
then concentrated with all its riches in this liturgy of

the night, which reaches its climax, after the period of Lent, in the first "Alleluia."

Alleluia: the cry that expresses paschal joy!

The exclamation that rings out again in the middle of the night of waiting and brings with it already the joy of the morning. It brings with it the certainty of resurrection. That which, at the first moment, the lips of the women in front of the sepulcher or the mouths of the apostles did not have the courage to utter, now the Church, thanks to their testimony, expresses with her Alleluia.

This song of joy, sung about midnight, announces to us the Great Day. (In some Slav languages, Easter is called the "Great Night"; after the Great Night there arrives the Great Day: "the day which the Lord has made").

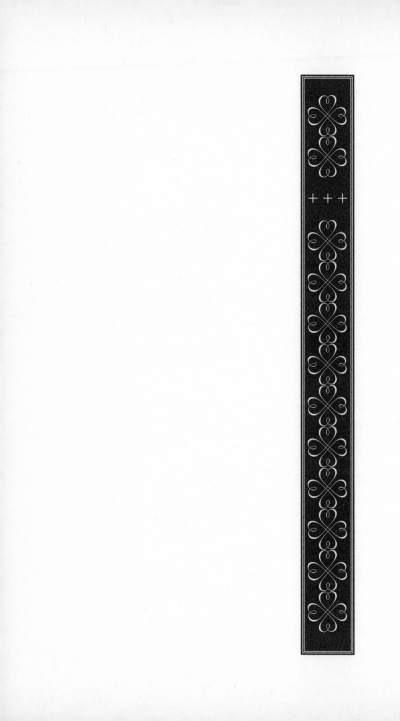

FIVE

Easter

THE MOST IMPORTANT DAY IN THE
CHRISTIAN YEAR

*I*T MAY SEEM SOMETIMES that Christmas has become the most important day of the year, but for many reasons, and according to the Christian calendar, Easter is the lynchpin for everything else. Our faith would make no sense if it were not for the events of Holy Week and Easter Sunday. It is on these days that we remember and participate in the most essential facts of life with God.

Easter is known as the "Feast of feasts," and the "Solemnity of solemnities." The promise of Easter began at Creation itself. As Pope Pius XI said in 1937: "The promise of a Redeemer brightens the first page of the history of mankind, and the confident hope aroused by this promise softened the keen regret for a paradise which had been lost. It was this hope that accompanied the human race on its weary journey, until in the fullness of time the expected Savior came." Then, of course, that expected Savior died, and on the third day, He rose again!

JESUS STOOD AMONG THEM

While they were talking about this, Jesus himself stood among them and said to them, "Peace be with you." They were startled and terrified, and thought that they were seeing a ghost.

(Lk. 24:36–7)

THE LORD, AS YOU HAVE HEARD, appeared to his disciples after his Resurrection, and greeted them, saying: "Peace be with you." This is indeed peace, and the salutation of salvation; for salutation receives its name from salvation. And what better than that Salvation Itself should greet humankind? For Christ is our salvation. He is our salvation who was wounded for us, and fastened with nails to the wood, and taken down from the wood and laid in the sepulcher. But he rose from the sepulcher, and though his wounds were healed the scars remained. All of this he judged necessary for his disciples, so that he would keep his scars to heal the wounds of their souls. What wounds are these? The wounds of their unbelief. For Christ appeared before their eyes, showing them a true body, but they believed they only saw a spirit.

—ST. AUGUSTINE OF HIPPO
from a sermon on Easter

"I go away, and I will come to you"

— POPE BENEDICT XVI —
Homily for the Easter Vigil Mass
March 22, 2008

*I*N HIS FAREWELL DISCOURSE, Jesus announced his imminent death and resurrection to his disciples with these mysterious words: "I go away, and I will come to you," he said (Jn. 14:28).

Dying is a "going away." Even if the body of the deceased remains behind, he himself has gone away into the unknown, and we cannot follow him (cf. Jn. 13:36). Yet in Jesus' case, there is something utterly new, which changes the world. In the case of our own death, the "going away" is definitive, there is no return. Jesus, on the other hand, says of his death: "I go away, and I will come to you." It is by going away that he comes. His going ushers in a completely new and greater way of being present. By dying he enters into the love of the Father. His dying is an act of love.

Love, however, is immortal. Therefore, his going away is transformed into a new coming, into a form of presence which reaches deeper and does not come to an end. During his earthly life, Jesus, like all of us, was tied to the external conditions of bodily existence: to a determined place and a determined time. Bodiliness places limits on our existence. We cannot be simultaneously in two different places. Our time is destined to come to an end. And between the "I" and the "you" there is a wall of otherness. To be sure, through love we can somehow enter the other's existence. Nevertheless, the insurmountable barrier of being different remains in place. Yet Jesus, who is now totally transformed through the act of love, is free from such barriers and limits. He is able not only to pass through closed doors in the outside world, as the Gospels recount (cf. Jn. 20:19). He can pass through the interior door separating the "I" from the "you," the closed door between yesterday and today, between the past and the future.

On the day of his solemn entry into Jerusalem, when some Greeks asked to see him, Jesus replied with the parable of the grain of wheat which has to pass through death in order to bear much fruit. In this way he foretold his own destiny: these words were not addressed simply to one or two Greeks in the space of a few minutes. Through his Cross, through his going away, through his dying like the grain of wheat, he would truly arrive among the Greeks, in such a way that they could see him and touch him through faith. His going away is transformed into a coming, in the Risen Lord's universal manner of presence, in which he is there yesterday, today and for ever, in which he embraces all times and all places. Now he can even surmount the wall of otherness that separates the "I" from the "you." This happened with Paul, who describes the process of his conversion and his Baptism in these words: "it is no longer I who live, but Christ who lives in me" (Gal. 2:20). Through the coming of the Risen One, Paul obtained a new identity. His closed "I" was opened. Now he lives in communion with Jesus Christ, in the great "I" of believers who have become—as he puts it—"one in Christ" (Gal. 3:28).

THE JOYFUL EASTER SERMON
OF ST. JOHN CHRYSOSTOM

*I*S THERE ANYONE who is a devout lover of God? Let them enjoy this beautiful bright festival! Is there anyone who is a grateful servant? Let them rejoice and enter into the joy of their Lord!

Are there any weary with fasting? Let them now receive their wages! If any have toiled from the first hour, let them receive their due reward. If any have come after the third hour, let him with gratitude join in the Feast! They that arrived after the sixth hour, let them not doubt, for they too will sustain no loss. If any delayed until the ninth hour, let them still not hesitate, but let them come, too. And they who arrived only at the eleventh hour, may they be unafraid to come.

For the Lord is gracious and receives the last even as the first. He gives rest to him that comes at the eleventh hour, as well as to him that toiled from the very beginning. He bestows his grace upon them all. He accepts the works as He greets the endeavor. The deed He honors and the intention He commends.

Let us all enter into the joy of the Lord!

First and last alike receive your reward; rich and poor, rejoice together! Sober and lazy, we all celebrate the day!

You that have kept the fast, and you that have not, rejoice today, for the Table is richly laid with God's goodness! Feast royally on it; the calf is a fatted one. Let no one go away hungry. Everyone partake of the cup of faith. Enjoy all the riches of His goodness!

Let no one grieve at his poverty, for the universal kingdom has been revealed. Let no one mourn that he has fallen again and again, for forgiveness has risen from the grave. Let no one fear death, for the Death of our Savior has set us free. He has destroyed it by enduring it.

He destroyed Hades when He descended into it. He put it into an uproar even as it tasted of His flesh. Isaiah foretold this when he said, "You, O Hell, have been troubled by encountering Him below." Hell was in an uproar because it was done away with. It was in an uproar because it was mocked. It was in an uproar, for it was destroyed. It was in an uproar, for it was annihilated.

It is in an uproar, for it is now made captive. Hell took a body, and discovered God. It took earth, and encountered Heaven. It took what it saw, and was overcome by what it did not see.

O death, where is thy sting? O Hades, where is thy victory?

Christ is risen, and you, death, are annihilated! Christ is risen, and the evil ones are cast down! Christ is risen, and the angels rejoice! Christ is risen, and life is liberated! Christ is risen, and the tomb is emptied of its dead. Christ, having risen from the dead, is become the firstfruits of those who have fallen asleep. To Him be Glory and Power forever and ever. Amen!

—ST. JOHN CHRYSOSTOM
from an Easter Sermon Given at Constantinople

A BENEDICTION *from*

POPE BENEDICT XVI

*T*HE EASTER PROCLAMATION spreads throughout the world with the joyful song of the Alleluia! Let
us sing it with our lips, and let us sing it above all with
our hearts and our lives, with a manner of life that is
unleavened, that is to say, simple, humble, and fruitful
in good works.

Christ my hope is risen, and he goes before you
into Galilee. The Risen One goes before us and he
accompanies us along the paths of the world. He is
our hope, He is the true peace of the world. Amen![3]

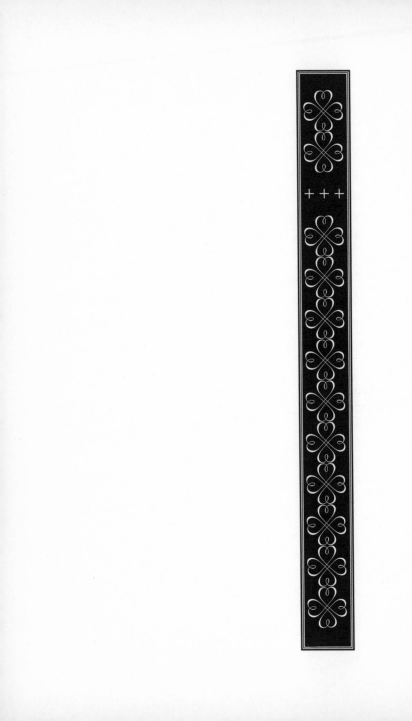

SIX

Eastertide

(*or* THE EASTER SEASON,
or PASCHAL TIME)

THE MEANING OF EASTERTIDE

*E*ASTERTIDE COVERS THE PERIOD of fifty days
from Easter Sunday to Pentecost Sunday. It corre-
sponds to a Jewish feast that was celebrated by the
first Christians. We read about this in the book of
Deuteronomy:

> Observe the month of Abib by keeping the passover
> to the LORD your God, for in the month of Abib the
> LORD your God brought you out of Egypt by night.
> You shall offer the passover sacrifice to the LORD your
> God, from the flock and the herd, at the place that
> the LORD will choose as a dwelling for his name. You
> must not eat with it anything leavened. For seven days
> you shall eat unleavened bread with it—the bread of
> affliction—because you came out of the land of Egypt
> in great haste, so that all the days of your life you may
> remember the day of your departure from the land of
> Egypt. No leaven shall be seen with you in all your
> territory for seven days; and none of the meat of what
> you slaughter on the evening of the first day shall
> remain until morning. You are not permitted to offer
> the passover sacrifice within any of your towns that
> the LORD your God is giving you. But at the place that
> the LORD your God will choose as a dwelling for his
> name, only there shall you offer the passover sacrifice,

in the evening at sunset, the time of day when you departed from Egypt. You shall cook it and eat it at the place that the LORD your God will choose; the next morning you may go back to your tents. For six days you shall continue to eat unleavened bread, and on the seventh day there shall be a solemn assembly for the LORD your God, when you shall do no work.

You shall count seven weeks; begin to count the seven weeks from the time the sickle is first put to the standing grain. Then you shall keep the festival of weeks to the LORD your God, contributing a freewill-offering in proportion to the blessing that you have received from the LORD your God.

—DEUTERONOMY 16:1–10

We Must Live Not for Ourselves, but for Christ, Who Died for Us

POPE ST. LEO THE GREAT
Homily on the Passion of Christ

LET US, THEN, confess what the blessed teacher of the nations, the Apostle Paul, confessed, saying, "Faithful is the saying, and worthy of all acceptation, that Christ Jesus came into the world to save sinners." For God's mercy towards us is all the more wonderful because Christ died not for the righteous or for the holy, but for the unrighteous and the wicked. Though the nature of the Godhead could not sustain the sting of death, at his birth he took from us that which he might offer for us. Long ago, God threatened our death with the power of his death, saying by the mouth of Hosea the prophet, "O death, I will be thy death, and I will be thy destruction, O hell."

By dying Christ underwent the laws of hell, but by rising again he broke them, and so destroyed the continuity of death as to make it temporal instead of eternal. "For as in Adam all die, even so in Christ shall all be made alive." And so, we should let come to pass what St. Paul spoke of: "that they that live, should henceforth not live to themselves but to Him who died for all and rose again." Because the old things have passed away and all things are become new, let none remain in this old carnal life, but let us all be renewed by daily progress and growth in devotion. For however much a man be justified, yet so long as he remains in this life, he can always be more approved and better. Anyone that is not advancing is actually going back, and the one that is gaining nothing is losing something.

Let's run, then, with the steps of faith, by the works of mercy, in the love of righteousness, that keeping the day of our redemption spiritually, "not in the old leaven of malice and wickedness, but in the unleavened bread of sincerity and truth," we may deserve to be partakers of Christ's resurrection, who with the Father and the Holy Ghost lives and reigns forever and ever. Amen.

NOTHING CAN SHOW THE VALUE which God sets on the souls of us more clearly than what the Incarnate Word has done for our redemption from sin and hell. "If," says St. Eucharius, "you do not believe your Creator, ask your Redeemer how precious you are." Speaking of the care that we ought to have for our brothers and sisters, St. Ambrose says, "The great value of the salvation of a brother is known from the death of Christ." We usually judge the value of something by the price we have paid for it. Now, Jesus Christ has, according to the Apostle Paul, purchased our very souls with His own Blood. "For you were bought with a price; therefore glorify God in your body" (1 Cor. 6:20). We can then say that the soul is of as much value as the Blood of a God. Such, indeed, is the language of St. Hilary: *"Tam copioso munere redemptio agitur, ut homo Deum valere videatur"* (So plentiful a redemption was given, that we might seem to be worth God). In this spirit, the Savior tells us: "Truly . . . just as you did it to one of the least of these who are members of my family, you did it to me" (Mt. 25:40).

—ST. ALPHONSUS LIGUORI

from a sermon on the Second Sunday of Easter

POPE ST. LEO THE GREAT
Homily on Meditating on Christ's Passion

TRUE REVERENCE for the Lord's passion means fixing the eyes of our heart on Jesus crucified and recognizing in him our own humanity.

The earth—and our earthly nature—should tremble at the suffering of its Redeemer. The rocks—and the hearts of unbelievers—should burst asunder. The dead, imprisoned in the tombs of their mortality, should come forth, the massive stones now ripped apart. Foreshadowings of the future resurrection should appear in the holy city, the Church of God: what is to happen to our bodies should now take place in our hearts.

No one, however weak, is denied a share in the victory of the cross. No one is beyond the help of the prayer of Christ. His prayer brought benefit to the multitude that raged against him. How much more does it bring to those who turn to him in repentance.

Ignorance has been destroyed, obstinacy has been overcome. The sacred blood of Christ has quenched the flaming sword that barred access to the tree of life. The age-old night of sin has given place to the true light.

The Christian people are invited to share the riches of paradise. All who have been reborn have the way open before them to return to their native land, from which they had been exiled. Unless indeed they close off for themselves the path that could be opened before the faith of a thief.

The business of this life should not preoccupy us with its anxiety and pride, so that we no longer strive with all the love of our heart to be like our Redeemer, and to follow his example. Everything that he did or suffered was for our salvation: he wanted his body to share the goodness of its head.

The Two Natures of Jesus Christ

THE NAME OF JESUS [in Latin] comprises two syllables, five letters, three vowels, and two consonants. The Name has two syllables because Jesus has two natures, which is to say human and divine. Divine from the Father from which He is born without any mother; human from His mother from whom He is born without a father. Indeed, there are two syllables in this one Name because He has two natures and is one person. And it should also be noted that the two consonants make it possible for the Name to be sounded. The three vowels in the Name point to the divinity of Christ which, while it is One in itself, is manifested in three persons, for there are three who give testimony to Him in heaven, the Father, the Word, and the Holy Spirit, and these three are one. The two consonants signify the twofold elements of Christ's humanity, namely His body and soul. These are not pronounced in isolation but in conjunction with the other letters, for these two elements are conjoined in the unity of His person. For just as the rational soul and flesh are united in man, so also God and man are united in one Christ.

The Source of All Good Things

POPE LEO XIII

from the encyclical Auspicato Concessum

JESUS CHRIST, THE LIBERATOR of humankind, is the everlasting and ever-flowing source of all the good things that come to us from the infinite bounty of God; so that He who has once saved the world is He who will save it throughout all ages. "For there is no other name under heaven given to mortals by which we must be saved" (Acts 4:12). If then the human race falls into sin, either through its natural propensities or through the faults of men, it is absolutely indispensable to have recourse to Jesus Christ and to recognize in Him the most powerful and the most sure means of salvation. For so great and so efficacious is its divine virtue that it is at once a refuge from all dangers and a remedy for all evils. And the cure is certain, if humankind returns to the profession of Christian doctrine and to the rules of life laid down by the Gospel.

Turn to God in Prayer

POPE PIUS IX

from the encyclical Cum Sancta Mater Ecclesia

Now when holy mother church is joyously celebrating the annual solemnity of the Paschal Sacrament, she reminds her faithful of the joyful message of peace, which the risen Jesus Christ, having conquered death and overthrown the tyranny of the evil one, frequently and lovingly announced to His apostles and disciples. . . . Christ at His birth announced His peace to men of good will through angels, and later, left His peace to His disciples. Because of our love and care for Catholic peoples, we cannot refrain from crying out again and again for peace.

And so We exhort you, to stir the faithful committed to your vigilance in view of your outstanding piety, to turn to God in prayer, so that He might grant His deeply desired peace to all. For the same reason We have ordered that public prayers be offered by all within the Papal Territories to the most kind Father of Mercies. Following the illustrious example of Our predecessors, We have decided to have recourse to your prayers and those of the whole Church. And so We ask that you order public prayers in your dioceses as soon as possible. Having implored the patronage of Mary, may your faithful strenuously beseech our merciful God to turn His wrath from us and banish war to the very ends of the earth. By doing this, He may illuminate all minds by His divine grace and inflame all hearts with the love of Christian peace. He may insure that all may be rooted in faith and love. These then would diligently keep His holy Commandments and humbly beseech His forgiveness for their sins. Turning aside from evil and doing good, they would walk in the ways of justice, exercise mutual charity among themselves and obtain salutary peace with God, with themselves, and with all men.

O SWEET JESUS: what is there sweeter than Thee? Sweet is Thy memory, sweeter than that of honey or any other object. Thy very name is a name of sweetness, a name of salvation. For what does the name of Jesus signify, if not Savior? Therefore good Jesus, for Thy own sake, be to us a Jesus; so that Thou who gave us the beginning of the sweetness of faith, might also give us hope and love, so that living in it we might die in Thee and come to Thee.

This name which is so holy and glorious is *quod invocatum est super nos*, "invoked over us," and is none other than that of which Peter spoke when he said, "there is no other name under heaven by which we can be saved."

St. Anthony of Padua (1195–1231) was a prominent Franciscan in the days immediately after the death of St. Francis of Assisi. His preaching was praised by Pope Gregory IX as "a jewel case of the Bible." Gregory IX canonized St. Anthony in 1232, and in 1946 Pope Pius XII declared him a Doctor of the Church.

NOTES

1 Pope John XXIII, *Paenitentiam Agere*, "Encyclical on the Need for the Practice of Interior and Exterior Penance," July 1, 1962.

2 Dom Gueranger, *The Liturgical Year: Lent* (Westminster, MD: The Newman Press, 1949).

3 Pope Benedict XVI, Mass of the Day, Easter Sunday, April 12, 2009.

ABOUT PARACLETE PRESS

Who We Are

Paraclete Press is a publisher of books, recordings, and DVDs on Christian spirituality. Our publishing represents a full expression of Christian belief and practice—from Catholic to Evangelical, from Protestant to Orthodox.

We are the publishing arm of the Community of Jesus, an ecumenical monastic community in the Benedictine tradition. As such, we are uniquely positioned in the marketplace without connection to a large corporation and with informal relationships to many branches and denominations of faith.

What We Are Doing

Books

Paraclete publishes books that show the richness and depth of what it means to be Christian. Although Benedictine spirituality is at the heart of all that we do, we publish books that reflect the Christian experience across many cultures, time periods, and houses of worship. We publish books that nourish the vibrant life of the church and its people—books about spiritual practice, formation, history, ideas, and customs.

We have several different series, including the best-selling Living Library, Paraclete Essentials, and Paraclete Giants series of classic texts in contemporary English; A Voice from the Monastery— men and women monastics writing about living a spiritual life today; award-winning literary faith fiction and poetry; and the Active Prayer Series that brings creativity and liveliness to any life of prayer.

Recordings

From Gregorian chant to contemporary American choral works, our music recordings celebrate sacred choral music through the centuries. Paraclete distributes the recordings of the internationally acclaimed choir Gloriæ Dei Cantores, praised for their "rapt and fathomless spiritual intensity" by *American Record Guide,* and the Gloriæ Dei Cantores Schola, which specializes in the study and performance of Gregorian chant. Paraclete is also the exclusive North American distributor of the recordings of the Monastic Choir of St. Peter's Abbey in Solesmes, France, long considered to be a leading authority on Gregorian chant.

DVDs

Our DVDs offer spiritual help, healing, and biblical guidance for life issues: grief and loss, marriage, forgiveness, anger management, facing death, and spiritual formation.

Learn more about us at our website:
www.paracletepress.com, or call us toll-free at 1-800-451-5006.